Dennis,

I'm gl[...]ed.
You ha[...]and
have k[...]derful
experiences. I hope you enjoy the stories
and messages in this book.

Soul Guide

4 Secrets Towards Mastering Life's Journey

Allen Rebenstorf

Cheers,

Allen Rebenstorf

Soul Guide

Printed by:
CreateSpace Independent Publishing Platform

Copyright © 2017, Allen Rebenstorf

Published in the United States of America

170119-00675.1

ISBN-13: 978-1548227180
ISBN-10: 1548227188

No parts of this publication may be reproduced without correct attribution to the author of this book.

For more information on 90-Minute Books including finding out how you can publish your own book, visit 90minutebooks.com or call (863) 318-0464

Here's What's Inside...

Soul Guide! 1

Chapter 1: "Confidence" - The Big "C" 4

Chapter 2: "Choose Happiness" 24

Chapter 3: "Learn Your Lessons" 37

Chapter 4: "Do the Right Thing" 51

We Are All Souls Having
a Human Experience 61

The 4 Secrets Towards Mastering
Life's Journey... 63

About The Author 64

Soul Guide!

Do you ever find yourself veering off track during your day? You know, you start off with good intentions and then—BAM—you find yourself down a rabbit hole taking a trip through negativity or scrolling Facebook into another realm? Then you wonder what happened in that time warp and how do you get back on track? Maybe something someone said or did ruins your whole day? Maybe you're feeling guilty because now you are late on a deadline. And, by the way, now you're late to pick up the kids from school. Does any of this sound familiar?

What if you had a secret formula to reset your mental state and emotions to get back on track quicker than ever before? We live in such a fast-paced world, with distractions coming at us 100 mph, nonstop. It's no wonder we lose track of what's important. It's no wonder we feel forced to take short cuts and end up making mistakes. If you feel this way, I'm here to tell you not to worry. You're not alone!

It doesn't matter if you're a child or an adult, we all deal with the same type of mania in our lives, just on different levels. This book provides a formula along with connective stories and crucial steps which just might change your life.

The concepts I share in this book started for me in the year 2000. I remember very clearly because it was a landmark year, a new millennium! Big changes, for better or worse, were expected and many felt the need to get prepared. All those zeros in the year, what will the computers do? You might remember those crazy mind games. There was no water left on store shelves, and a lot of people were certain planes were going to fall out of the sky, and we were going to be living back like a cave man.

Then it happened; "The 4 Secrets" came to me during a profound meditation. It was all crystal clear at that "ah ha" moment. I set out to think about how to shape this formula, so my kids will "get it" and remember it and, more importantly, use it effectively.

Kids love secrets, so that made it easier. The idea also needed to be shared in a simple and concise way so it could easily be recalled and uploaded into their brains at a moment's notice. Something as simple as 1234 would be perfect

Here is the framework:

Secret 1 is summed up one word: Confidence

Secret 2 is two words: Choose Happiness

Secret 3 is three words: Learn your lessons

Secret 4 is four words: Do the Right Thing

Little did I know that these 10 words had the power to change lives of all ages.

The human brain is wired to react to one's perceived circumstances quickly. The most common result is people give their power away and freely allow other people and other things to dictate how they feel, act, or react at any given time. Take a look at what happened during and after the election of Donald Trump. The media circus was one of perpetual crisis and hysteria causing good intelligent people on both sides of the vote to become hateful towards one another. The firestorm of character assaults and blame continues to this day for many people.

The purpose of the book is to help people become aware of their unawareness and take responsibility in their life. It demonstrates how to filter out potentially damaging thoughts. By applying these four key secrets, people can refresh their mind with a new perspective.

This book will take you on a journey of real life experiences as well as provide specific steps you can use to take back some of that mischievous mind control which comes and goes in our lives every day. It will also reference movie and book messages you may remember and may now link to "The 4 Secrets".

Enjoy the book!

I hope it provides you with the tools and mindsets to break through mental limitations and find clarity in times of confusion.

To Your Success!

Allen Rebenstorf

Chapter 1:
"Confidence" - The Big "C"

In *The Empire Strikes Back*, when Yoda is training Luke to be a Jedi, he demonstrates the power of the Force by raising an X-wing fighter from a swamp. Luke mutters, "I don't believe it." Yoda replies, "That is why you fail."

For many, the XIII Winter Olympic Games held in 1980 will stand out as one of the greatest defining moments in US sports history. Composed of collegiate and amateur athletes, the US hockey team was up against the well-developed and legendary players of the Soviet Union who had won the gold in the past four Olympics. On top of their Olympic triumphs, the Soviets beat the US team 10–3 in an exhibition match earlier that month, so the Soviets were the favorites to win it all again.

The US team entered the games seeded seventh out of twelve teams which qualified for the games. After a surprising start with a 2–2 tie against Sweden followed by a 7–3 victory against a very powerful Czechoslovakia team, the American team finished 4 and 0 with 1 draw to advance them to the medal round. Knowing what the US boys were up against, the Team USA coach Herb Brooks delivered a life changing speech just before game time which gave the team USA the confidence and personal belief mindset they needed to make history. Here is what Herb said...

"Great moments... are born from great opportunity. And that's what you have here, tonight, boys. That's what you've earned here tonight. One game. If we played 'em ten times, they might win nine. But not this game. Not tonight. Tonight, we skate with them. Tonight, we stay with them. And we shut them down because we can! Tonight, WE are the greatest hockey team in the world. You were born to be hockey players. Every one of you. And you were meant to be here tonight. This is your time. Their time is done. It's over. I'm sick and tired of hearing about what a great hockey team the Soviets have. Screw 'em. This is your time. Now go out there and take it."

At the end of the first period, the game was tied 2–2. The Soviets edged up 3–2 by the end of the second period. Then came the famous third period. Mark Johnson tied the game 3–3 and brought team USA back for good. With ten minutes left in the game, Mike Eruzione scored the infamous fourth and winning goal along with Jim Craig's outstanding play at the net, and the US team defeated the Soviets 4–3.

As the final seconds counted down, announcer Al Michaels said, "Do you believe in miracles?" as the final horn sounded. Team USA believed that night even though nobody else did. Then the chants began...

If you listen closely, you may still be able to hear the echo of those chants: "U.S.A. ... U.S.A!!"

> *"If you hear a voice within you say 'you cannot paint,' then by all means paint, and that voice will be silenced."*
>
> -Vincent Van Gogh

True confidence is very different from egotistical swagger. When people believe in themselves and their abilities without bravado, there are certain things they simply don't do.

This section was inspired by:
Author, Travis Bradberry - co-author of the best-selling book, Emotional Intelligence

10 Things Confident People Don't Do

1. **They don't make excuses.**
If there's one trait confident people have in spades, it's self-efficacy—the belief they can make things happen. It's about having an internal locus of control rather than an external one. That's why you won't hear confident people blaming traffic for making them late or an unfair boss for their failure to get a promotion. Confident people don't make excuses because they believe they're in control of their lives.

2. **They don't quit.**
Confident people don't give up the first time something goes wrong. They see both problems and failures as obstacles to overcome rather than impenetrable barriers to success. That doesn't mean they keep trying the same thing over and over. One of the first things confident people do when something is to figure out why it went wrong and how they can prevent it the next time.

3. **They don't wait for permission to act.**
Confident people don't need somebody to tell them what to do or when to do it. They don't waste time asking themselves questions like "Can I?" or "Should I?" If they ask themselves anything, it's, "Why wouldn't I?" Whether it's running a meeting when the chairperson doesn't show up or going the extra mile to solve a customer's problem, it doesn't even occur to them to wait for somebody else to take care of it. They see what needs to be done, and they do it.

4. **They don't seek attention.**
People are turned off by those who are desperate for attention. Confident people know that being yourself is much more effective than trying to prove you're important. People catch on to your attitude quickly and are more attracted to the right attitude than what, or how many, people you know. Confident people always seem to bring the right attitude. Confident people are masters of attention diffusion. When they're receiving attention for an accomplishment, they quickly shift the focus to all the people who worked hard to help get them there. They don't crave approval or praise because they draw their self-worth from within.

5. **They don't need constant praise.**
Have you ever been around somebody who constantly needs to hear how great he or she is? Confident people don't do that. It goes back to that internal locus of control. They don't think their success is dependent on other people's approval, and they understand that, no matter how well they perform, there's always going to be somebody out there offering nothing but criticism. Confident people also know the kind of confidence dependent on praise from other people isn't confidence at all; it's narcissism.

6. **They don't put things off.**
Why do people procrastinate? Sometimes it's simply because they're lazy. A lot of times, though, it's because they're afraid—that is, afraid of change, failure or maybe even success.

Confident people don't put things off. Because they believe in themselves and expect their actions will lead them closer to their goals, they don't sit around waiting for the right time or the perfect circumstances. They know today is the only time that matters. If they think it's not the right time, they make it the right time.

7. **They don't pass judgment.**
Confident people don't pass judgment on others because they know everyone has something to offer, and they don't need to take other people down a notch to feel good about themselves. Comparing yourself to other people is limiting. Confident people don't waste time sizing people up and worrying about whether or not they measure up to everyone they meet.

8. **They don't avoid conflict.**
Confident people don't see conflict as something to be avoided at all costs; they see it as something to manage effectively. They don't go along to get along, even when that means having uncomfortable conversations or making unpleasant decisions. They know conflict is part of life and they can't avoid it without cheating themselves out of the good stuff, too.

9. **They don't let a lack of resources get in their way.**
Confident people don't get thrown off course just because they don't have the right title, the right staff or the money to make things happen. Either

they find a way to get what they need, or they figure out how to get by without it.

10. **They don't get too comfortable.**
Confident people understand getting too comfortable is the mortal enemy of achieving their goals. That's because they know comfort leads to complacency, and complacency leads to stagnation. When they start feeling comfortable, they take that as a big red flag and start pushing their boundaries again so they can continue to grow as both a person and a professional. They understand a little discomfort is a good thing.

Embracing the behaviors of confident people is a great way to increase your odds of success, which, in turn, will lead to more confidence. The science is clear; now you just have to decide to act on it.

The Power of Confidence
There was a business executive who was deep in debt and could see no way out. Creditors were closing in on him. Suppliers were demanding payment. He sat on the park bench, head in hands, wondering if anything could save his company from bankruptcy. Suddenly, an old man appeared before him. "I can see that something is troubling you," he said. After listening to the executive's woes, the old man said, "I believe I can help you." He asked the man his name, wrote out a check, and pushed it into his hand saying, "Take this money. Meet me here exactly one year from today, and you can pay me back at that

time." Then he turned and disappeared as quickly as he had come.

The business executive saw in his hand a check for $500,000, signed by John D. Rockefeller, then one of the richest men in the world! "I can erase my money worries in an instant!" he realized. But instead, the executive decided to put the uncashed check in his safe. Just knowing it was there might give him the strength to work out a way to save his business, he thought. With renewed optimism, he negotiated better deals and extended terms of payment. He closed several big sales. Within a few months, he was out of debt and making money once again.

Exactly one year later, he returned to the park with the uncashed check. At the agreed-upon time, the old man appeared. But just as the executive was about to hand back the check and share his success story, a nurse came running up and grabbed the old man. "I'm so glad I caught him!" she cried. "I hope he hasn't been bothering you. He's always escaping from the rest home and telling people he's John D. Rockefeller. Then she led the old man away by the arm.

The astonished executive just stood there, stunned. All year long he'd been wheeling and dealing, buying and selling, convinced he had half a million dollars behind him. Suddenly, he realized it wasn't the money, real or imagined, which had turned his life around. It was his newfound self-confidence which gave him the power to achieve anything he went after.

The Importance of Being Confident

As a Real Estate Consultant in Phoenix, Arizona, I've had the good fortune of helping many different people over the years. During the market crash, I helped a very successful business owner in Arizona buy some investment properties. I remember feeling a little intimidated by the success and wealth of this particular client. I thought, "Who am I to help this person with his investment portfolio? He probably makes more in a day than I do all year."

At times, I questioned my confidence in providing the best possible advice because of his status. The thing which stands out most from this experience was with each deal before he would sign the contract, he looked me in the eyes and said, "Tell me I'm doing the right thing."

The first time, I probably looked like a deer in the headlights. And, in my less-than-confident voice, repeated, "I believe you're doing the right thing."

The more transactions we did, the more confidently I repeated, "You're doing the right thing," each time he asked.

To this day, I'm not sure if he did that for my sake or his. While he benefited by hundreds of thousands during that period, I benefited mentally, for which I am most grateful to this day. That was a turning point in my awareness of the importance of being confident and showing it.

Have you ever wondered what it is about certain people which attract us to them so quickly while not knowing a thing about them? Perhaps you've seen someone you didn't even know and thought, "Wow, that person has it going on," not because of the clothes they were wearing or the car they were driving, but just the air about them.

I've noticed this several times, and as much as I try to put my finger on what it is they do to create that sense of intrigue, I struggle with identifying the magic ingredients. Someone once said people are secretly seeking to be led. Good leaders naturally project confidence because they are clear on what they want, where they're going, and how they are getting there. Getting clarity can be one of the greatest gifts you can give yourself.

Confidence Let's You Go the Distance

Who hasn't seen the movie, *Rocky*? To this day, the theme song, "Eye of the Tiger," clears my head and fires me up.

Rocky was a slightly dimwitted amateur boxer from Philadelphia's tough neighborhood. He lived a life of hard knocks until he gets a surprise chance of a lifetime to fight the world heavyweight champion as a goodwill gesture. The Champ, Apollo Creed, is undefeated, never even knocked down in the ring. No one has ever even gone the distance with the champ. Apollo oozes confidence and lives the seemingly perfect life. He is unquestionably the king of the ring, and nobody else can even come close to his skill level.

Rocky survives round after round being heavily battered by the champ. Then with one mighty punch, Rocky sends Apollo to the mat for the first time in his career. The crowd is stunned. This fight was supposed to be a slam dunk. The best fighter in the world against a nobody from the streets of Philadelphia. Even though Rocky had been outpunched 10 to 1, that one powerful punch made his confidence soar.

Rocky knew Apollo could be taken down and he fought to the bitter end, going the distance. The crowd went crazy. A new boxing hero was born.

Even though Rocky lost on points. He had done two things to the champ which had never been done before—knocked him down and went the distance.

Rocky didn't believe in himself until he knocked Apollo to the mat. Then he believed he deserved to be in that ring. Nothing changed, he just believed in himself, and his confidence exploded. Everyone couldn't help but feel that energy of the big "C" that night.

Confidence is one of those things which can either propel you forward to achieve your dreams or hold you back for fear of failure. Everyone faces this issue, to some extent, at some point in their lives. The questions become, "How confident are you? When do you feel the most confident? How can you build that confidence in times when you need it?" Confidence is important for most people in most situations. If you're lacking confidence, it can be difficult to get up the courage to go after what you want, whether it's giving a presentation at work, asking someone to be your mentor, or volunteering for a committee at your child's school. It impacts people everywhere.

There are two main elements which make up confidence: self-efficacy and self-esteem. When we have a sense of self-efficacy, we have the belief that, if we work hard in a certain area, we will be able to achieve our goals. This belief helps us take on difficult tasks and keep working through obstacles when we face them. When we have high self-efficacy, we are working in what Stanford Professor Carol Dweck, author of *Mindset: The New Psychology of Success*, calls our growth mindset.

Self-esteem is essentially what we think and feel about ourselves, a judgment of our self-worthiness. Our esteem of ourselves is a predictor of relevant outcomes such as job performance, academic achievements or personal habits. Expert Nathaniel Branden defines self-esteem as "the experience of being competent to cope with the basic challenges of life and being worthy of happiness."

Some people have such healthy levels of confidence, they are bordering on arrogance. Others have a cripplingly low level, which impacts every aspect of their lives. And research tells us women are prone to lower levels of confidence than men. In the recent *The Atlantic* cover story "The Confidence Gap," highly respected journalists and authors Katty Kay and Claire Shipman reported, "Under qualified and underprepared men don't think twice about leaning in. Overqualified and over prepared, too many women still hold back. Women feel confident only when they are perfect. Or practically perfect."

Even those who are brimming with confidence in some areas of their lives can be much less so in others. Take Oprah Winfrey, for example. Most people would look at Oprah with her commanding presence and global platform and think such a woman would never have a crisis of confidence. But even Oprah herself has stated that while she thrives on stage in front of thousands speaking on matters of the heart, emotions, and finding your purpose, give her a problem of a mathematical or technical nature, and her confidence goes straight out the window.

The important point to remember is it's not an all-or-nothing game. The good news is you can build confidence, both in yourself and in others.

Here are five areas you can start working on today to help establish and build your confidence so it can have a positive effect on every area of your life.

1. **Take stock**

Often when we lack confidence, we have forgotten about our achievements, the great things we have accomplished, and skills we have developed which make us who we are. Our brains are wired for negativity, meaning we have a bias to focus on the problems in our lives and what can go wrong. This is great when we need to run away from danger, like that bear in the woods, but not so helpful when we are about to give a major presentation or a speech at the local school. When you feel less than confident about your abilities, take some time to write down a list of your recent wins, things you have done which you are proud of or other people have commented on. It could be anything from the dinner party you hosted on Saturday night to finishing your book or PhD. It is also helpful to write down a list of your skills so you can reflect on them next time you feel that wave of negativity crashing down on you.

2. **Focus on your strengths**

Just like we are wired for negativity, we are also geared toward looking at our weaknesses rather than our strengths. There has been significant work done over the past twenty years, pioneered by the Gallup organization, around what happens when we focus on and use our strengths instead of our weaknesses. Our strengths are those things we are good at and enjoy doing. They give us a rush of energy and take us into the state of flow, where we lose time because we are so absorbed in what we are doing. When we use our strengths, our wellbeing, happiness, productivity, and engagement at work all increase. When we feel less than confident, it can be all too easy to start honing in on our weaknesses. When you need a boost of confidence, try instead to pick one of your strengths and use that to propel you forward. The more you can use your strengths in your days, the greater your confidence will be and the more it will build over time. There is a great free character strengths test you can take through the VIA Institute at viacharacter.org.

3. **Watch for your triggers**

Often when we feel our confidence waning, or when it just disappears altogether, there is usually a trigger which sets us off. By trying to pinpoint those moments where we feel undermined, we can learn to short-circuit them at the gate. Think of these situations as examples: it's Monday morning and you have overslept, raced out the door without breakfast and you barely had time to run a brush through your hair, let alone find the right jacket for your suit. You arrive feeling less than fabulous when your boss calls a meeting where you need to update her on your latest project. Not feeling great about yourself, you do a less than stellar job and walk out feeling dejected. The trigger here was being rushed and not being physically put together in a way that instilled confidence in yourself (and in others, no doubt). Or think about this one: you have that friend who always seems to make a comment about you which gets under your skin just the right amount to leave you feeling undermined and less than sure of yourself. This is another trigger which can zap your confidence. Work out what your triggers are, then set strategies in place to either ensure they don't happen, or to fast track your way past them.

4. **Change your story**
A few interrelated things which dramatically impact our confidence is our negative self-talk, our self-limiting beliefs and the stories we tell ourselves. We have somewhere between 60,000 to 80,000 thoughts a day. When you start to tune into them, it can be astonishing to notice just how many of those thoughts are negative stories about ourselves we would be just horrified if anyone actually heard articulated. Yet we allow these stories to ramble around inside our heads, impacting everything we do. When we can start to tune in to our negative self-talk, understand where our self-limiting beliefs are coming from, hear the story and learn to change it when it is not helpful, we can radically impact our confidence levels and even change our lives. Build quiet time into your days through meditation or mindfulness practice, so you can

tune in and start to discern the voices. When you hear a story or a belief coming up, the first and most helpful question to ask yourself is, "Is this true?" If it is true and it's helpful, then there's no problem. But if it's not, think about what a more helpful and confidence raising story could be and go with that instead. By doing this over time, you will create new stories which will help you, not harm you.

5. **Build your support network**

Who do you have in your corner, who is your best cheerleader? Who in your workplace is your greatest advocate? And which of your friends or family do you love spending time with because they make you feel so great about yourself? Hopefully, you have someone in your life who makes you feel like the very best version of yourself. You just feel that little bit taller, brighter, and shinier when you are around them. These are the type of people you want to surround yourself with as much as possible, and certainly they are the people you want to call when you need a boost of confidence. Think about who in your life can play the role of cheerleader and supporter. It could be your best friend, your boss, your mom, father, or even your child. When you need that little extra boost before a job interview, a big meeting, or perhaps even a date, your support team can be invaluable to help get you through. If you don't have someone you can call on or they aren't available at your critical moment, then build yourself a confidence toolkit. Your toolkit could include a favorite song you blast as loud as you can and dance around your living room. It could be a favorite piece of clothing or pair of shoes which make you feel great. Or it could be that fabulous red lipstick or spicy aftershave. Have these things ready and on hand when you need them. Then, even if you do have your best friend on speed dial, having your favorite things ready to go can only add to your confidence inducing state. The more tools, the merrier.

Confidence is a muscle you can build. It doesn't matter where you are starting from, just that you move forward with positive intention and know the direction in which you are going. Start small. Little successes in increasing your confidence can make a big difference over time, and you will grow as you go. Use the strategies here and you may find that, over time, your confidence blooms like a beautiful rose, and it will be a magical sight to behold for all around you.

The following questions can help you strengthen your confidence:

1. When you feel most confident, what are you doing?

2. When you feel you lack confidence, what are the triggers? Try and pinpoint the moments or situations which undermine your confidence and write them down.

3. Our confidence often suffers due to stories we tell ourselves. What stories of yours come up when you lack confidence?

4. When you have identified your story, ask yourself, "Is this true?" and write down your answers. Do this for each story you have identified as a confidence robber.

5. What are the new stories you need to create for yourself which will replace the old limiting beliefs?

6. Write down a list of your achievements, skills, and key wins over the past 12 months. Use this as a source of strength when you need a confidence boost.

7. Who in your support system sees you as the best version of yourself? How can you utilize these people as a resource when you need a confidence boost?

8. What are some of the small things you can integrate into your day to give yourself a boost? Think about things which add to your confidence like getting your hair or makeup done, eating right, exercising, being grateful for the good things in your life, or helping someone out.

This section was inspired by:
Author, Megan Dalla-Camina

Chapter 2:
"Choose Happiness"

> *"Success is not the key to happiness. Happiness is the key to success. If you love what you are doing, you will be successful."*

-Albert Schweitzer

> *"Count your rainbows, not your thunderstorms."*

-Alyssa Knight

Story 1

It occurred to me as a young father that the happiness of my children seemed to be dependent on the happiness in their environment. If their friends were happy, they were happy, too, and vice versa.

I remember when my daughter was in grade school, she was excited to tell me about the bookmobile coming to school the next day and she could buy books. As the pushover father I was at the time, I agreed to give her money to buy some books. The following day came and she was thrilled to be going to school and shop the bookmobile. However, she discovered some of her friends were unhappy because their parents did not give them money to buy books. This, in turn, made her unhappy. So she thought about how she could make them happy. Then she came up with a solution. She would give her friends the money she had to buy books. So her friends bought books and she was happy for them. Upon returning home from a hard day's work, I asked my daughter what books she bought from the bookmobile and she told me none. I asked her why not, and she explained her friends didn't have money to buy books and they were sad, so she gave them her money. She then informed me of the good news that the bookmobile would be at school the next day, too, so she would need some more money to buy books for herself. As I tried to sort out what just happened in my own mind, besides being played, it hit me. She knew I would give her more money and everyone would be happy, at least for the time being.

Story 2

A couple years later, I experienced another lesson about the happiness barometer. My daughter excelled at gymnastics at an early age. During her first competitive season, she became a stand out gymnast on the team. When the state meet came around that year, she had had the good fortune of doing outstanding performances in every event. Unfortunately, her teammates did not fare so well. She medaled in every event and each time, after coming back to her teammates from the podium, she tried to give them her medal, another version of the bookmobile solution. However, her teammates would not accept them from her, so she just put them away in her bag. To watch this happen, time and time again, was heartbreaking. I wanted her to be proud and happy. She had just won her first state championship! But she wanted nothing to do with it. If her teammates couldn't be happy, then she couldn't be happy either. We wanted to take her out for a special dinner to celebrate, but she was done. She chose to be in state of unhappiness because her teammates felt unhappy. That evening, instead of going to dinner, my daughter went to her room and made each of her teammates special cards encouraging them and thanking them for being great friends and teammates. The next day, she delivered the cards along with personal gifts to the girls. That's when I saw the second secret in action: happiness is a choice!

Story 3:
Movie: *The Pursuit of Happyness*

The main character, Chris Gardner, is a struggling single father. He gets evicted from his apartment with his young son, and they find themselves alone with no place to go. Even though Chris eventually lands a job as an intern at a prestigious brokerage firm, the position pays no money. The pair must live in shelters and endure many hardships, but Chris refuses to give in to despair as he struggles to create a better life for himself and his son.

Chris learned happiness is a choice. One of the signature lines in the movie is, "If people can't do something for themselves, they want to tell you, 'You can't do it.' If you want something, go get it, period." You can have happiness every day. It's your choice, nobody else's.

Turn off the news

I stopped watching the news many years ago. It seemed so doom-and-gloom. The negativity affected my own wellbeing. I knew there was plenty of good news to report on, but what came through loud and clear every day was the bad news. I found myself wondering if the media was trying to control the mindset of the people by focusing on bad news. If so, why would they do that. Is it because they know fear controls people and the media wants the power to control our lives. Look at the hysteria created by the election of Donald Trump and all the misinformation generated on both sides. The mainstream media clearly had a favorite in the race, as did the right wing media. The personal bashing and twisting of information became blatantly irresponsible, leaving people to select from the lesser of two evils. Everyone watched their friends and family tear each other apart on Facebook because they felt the other voted on the wrong side. I still ask myself, "Was this turmoil intentionally created by the media. Could this be the result they were after?" Again, the lesson here is we have a choice to get caught up in the hysterics and let it ruin our lives or choose the better option which includes love, compassion, gratitude, forgiveness, and ultimately, happiness. I'll take a second helping of happiness, please.

Joy is the Organic State of Your Soul
Some of us are born smiling; most of us must work at it. This may take learning some new techniques and unlearn some old mental habits—but the joyful news from the frontiers of science and psychology is mood is malleable, and happiness is yours for the choosing

1. **I know who I am, and I like myself.**
Happiness is your original nature. It is what you first experienced before you began to identify with a body, a family role, some school grades, your nationality, your business card, your Social Security number, and any other labels you keep. True happiness is being faithful to your true nature. The better you know yourself—what it is you love, what inspires you, what you are made of—the happier you will be. When you forget who you are, something very strange happens. You begin to search for happiness!

Happiness is your spiritual DNA. It is what you experience when you accept yourself, when you relax and when you stop obsessing about being a "size zero," about "why he hasn't called," and about "what I should be doing with my life." You will increase your happiness score significantly if you can begin to accept the happiness you hope to get after you find your true partner, get the dream job, buy the ideal home, and earn the right money, is already in you.

Joy is the organic state of your soul. It is not something you achieve. It is something you accept.

2. Why it's important to connect with others.
Relationships are the heart of happiness. Social research has found "rich and satisfying relationships" are the only external factors which will move your happiness score from "quite happy" to "very happy." A common mistake we make is to get so busy pursuing happiness we fail to give our best time, energy, and attention to our relationships. Remind yourself daily happiness is in the connections you make, in the friendships you keep, and in the love which exists between others.

If you want to be happy, be a friend. Identify your most important relationships, and think about how you can be a true friend to your partner, to your children, to your parents, to your colleagues, to your clients, etc. Another way to increase your happiness score is to make a conscious commitment to being the most loving person you can be. Your intention to love and be loved is the absolute key to happiness. Love is the most fun you can have with anyone. In the final analysis, there is no difference between happiness and love.

3. **Do what you love for a living.**
Today's workplaces are a modern tragedy in which too many people go to work without a sense of joy and love. "The biggest mistake

people make in life is not trying to make a living at doing what they most enjoy," Malcolm Forbes of *Forbes* magazine said. In the United States, only 50% of employees say they are satisfied with their work. You can increase your happiness score by making your work more purpose-centered. Start with identifying what real success is, what your real value is, how you can be more creative, and how you can enjoy yourself more.

The more you can say, "I love my work," and mean it, the higher your happiness score will be. People who love their work usually feel they are making a significant contribution to a cause they believe in. Reflect, therefore, on what you most want to contribute to your work and life overall. Remember, you are not here just to find happiness; you are here to extend it. You are inspiration-packed, wisdom-infused, made with love and blessed with talents. Look around today and give what is needed, give what appears to be missing, and give what your joy to give is.

4. **Have a good attitude.**

From zero to 10, how happy have you decided to be today? Is your score 5 out of 10, or 2 out of 10, or 8 out of 10, perhaps? Can you find the place in your mind where you have already made a decision about how good today will be, how good this year will be, and how good your life will be? Choice is a powerful thing. More of anything or everything will not make a difference to your happiness score until you consciously choose to be happy. Therefore, set an intention to be happy today. Decide to make today even more enjoyable than you thought it was going to be.

During "Be Happy," my eight-week happiness program, I ask my students this question: Could you be even happier even if nothing in the world around you changed? What is your answer: yes or no? In the most recent class, the score was 100% for "yes." How could this be? Well, common answers include, "I could choose to accept myself more," and, "I could choose to see things differently," and, "I could choose to enjoy my life more," and, "I could start making smarter choices." The one thing all these answers have in common is choice. Your happiness score rises when you stop chasing happiness and start choosing happiness.

5. **Appreciate your life.**
There are two meta-attitudes which can significantly increase your happiness score. The first is gratitude. The miracle of gratitude is it shifts your perception to such an extent it changes the world you see. Before you practice gratitude, you are in the dark, and there appears to be very little to be grateful for. Once you begin, new light dawn, sometimes a brilliant light, light as bright as heaven itself. Gratitude changes your brain—and it changes the world. The more you practice gratitude, the more you will find to be grateful for.

The real gift of gratitude is the more grateful you are, the more present you become. In the English language, the word "present" has three distinct meanings: "here," "now," and "a gift." This is surely not a coincidence. Practicing gratitude teaches you the greatest gifts are always available to you here and now! One way to practice gratitude is to start expressing it. Think about who you are truly grateful for in your life. Do you realize how happy they will be when you tell them? Gratitude is double happiness because it blesses both the giver and the receiver.

6. **Let go of your hurt and disappointment.**
Happiness is easy and natural until you experience your first wound. For this reason, the second meta-attitude which makes such a big difference to your happiness score is forgiveness. You cannot hold onto a grievance and be happy. Why? One reason is you can't be a victim and be happy. Holding onto a grievance is a sign of a mistaken identity. You are not a victim. Holding onto a grievance is a decision to keep suffering. Forgiveness helps you let go and be happy.

Resentment keeps you stuck in the past; forgiveness brings you back to the present. Resentment costs too much, and it doesn't make you happy. Resentment is a ball and chain; forgiveness sets you free again. Forgiveness offers you insurance against premature aging, a blocked heart, an unhealed past and an unhappy future. To increase your happiness score, try this forgiveness prayer:

Dear God, I declare today a day of amnesty, in which I gratefully volunteer to hand in all of my resentments and grievances to You. Please help me to handle well all of the peace that must inevitably follow. Amen.

7. **Do you know how to have fun?**

To be truly happy, you have to get your head around the idea that circumstances don't matter as much as you think they do. Happiness research studies reveal consistently that most people who score high levels of happiness do not experience markedly better life circumstances. So why are they so happy? Well, one answer is they know how to enjoy their life.

"Most of the time, I don't have very much fun, and the rest of the time I have no fun at all," quipped director Woody Allen. Good humor always has an element of truth in it. We're so preoccupied with the pursuit of happiness we are in danger of forgetting how to enjoy our lives. We promise ourselves, and each other, we will enjoy life more after we are happy. Go figure!

Note to self: Remember to enjoy the miracle of existence today. You can increase your happiness score immediately by being more spontaneous today. Disengage the autopilot, switch off the controls, stop being so sensible, issue a friendly restraining order to your superego, and for God's sake, let yourself have some fun today.

8. **Take care of your health and well-being.**
You cannot neglect yourself and find happiness. One of the side effects of chasing happiness is you become estranged from yourself. The quicker you chase, the faster time passes and the more difficult it is to locate yourself in your life. When you don't stop, you press on in hopes you will catch up with yourself somewhere down the line. But all the while, you keep leaving yourself behind. Something has to give.

Make some time for yourself today. Check in with yourself. Catch up on your news. Listen to your heart and to how you feel. Give yourself some of your best attention. Stop trying to be strong, and to be positive, and to keep going and simply be honest with yourself. Ask yourself, "What are my needs right now?" And, "How can I be kind to myself today?" In all my years of psychotherapy, I have never met a person who suffered from being too kind to herself.

The better you treat yourself, the better your happiness score will be.

9. **Get in touch with your spirituality.**
If you are committed to a spiritual path in your life, you are twice as likely to say you are "very happy," according to psychology research. Spirituality gives you a context for your life which is greater than your ego can see. The ego, which is your self-image, is based on an optical delusion of separation. Its outlook is: Everything Good's Outside. A strong spiritual faith helps you

to connect to what is real, to what is here now, and to what has already been given to you.

A daily spiritual practice you enjoy doing will help to increase your happiness score. The essential aim of any spiritual practice—be it meditation, prayer, yoga, tai chi, etc.—is to help you remove the blocks to the awareness of the happiness which already exists in the center of you. Spirituality connects you to your "being", so you don't get lost in going, doing, and having. It helps you to identify with the idea the soul is joy and to realize you are what you seek.

10. **How do you view happiness?**
Some things never change: Your greatest opportunity for healing and happiness has been, will be, still is, now! Since time began, spiritual teachers have taught their students to "be here and now," to "enjoy the moment," and to "seize the day." And since time began, spiritual students have repeatedly disregarded their teachers' wisdom at first. Like the Prodigal Son, we all eventually return to "now" to find our spiritual home and to find true happiness.

Living in the "not now" is a chief cause of unhappiness, pain, and lack. We do it because we fear happiness is somewhere else. The strain of not being present in your life is simply too great. When you miss out on the present, you miss out on so much. No now; no life. The good news is, however, it is never too late to be present and to show up in your life. Your happiness score increases the more present you are in your life.

> Truth is here, inspiration is here, love is here, peace is here, help is here, God is here, joy is here, because you are.

In the end, happiness is a choice—the frame through which we choose to see. The larger the frame, the more vivid the picture. The more we remember life is a gift, the happier we will be.

This section was inspired by:
www.oprah.com/spirit/How-to-Choose-Happiness and Robert Holden, PhD

Chapter 3: "Learn Your Lessons"

> *"Some people come into your life as blessings. Others come into your life as lessons."*
>
> -Mother Teresa
>
> *"Live as if you were to die tomorrow. Learn as if you were to live forever."*
>
> -Mahatma Gandhi

Look for lessons all the time, not just after a mistake. Did something go well today? Look for the lessons. What do we need to repeat to get those results again? What do we need to do differently to avoid those results? You will become a more intentional learner when you ask yourself these types of questions more regularly.

When you imagine everything happens for a reason, the questions you ask yourself become more profound:

- What is my lesson in this?
- What did I do right?
- What could I have done better?
- What will I do the next time I face that situation?

There is always a lesson in our daily life experiences, large and small. There is no guarantee we will learn from them. The learning only comes with reflection and the right questions.

Yoga teacher—Amarjit Singh
Your life purpose and life lessons may be considered the starting points for all your patterns. Consciously and unconsciously you create an environment to fulfill your purpose and learn your lesson. The more conscious you are of this process, the better equipped you are to understand and change your patterns of living to be in alignment with your soul's intention. When you examine ALL patterns from the perspective of your purpose and lesson, they are easy to understand.

If our most-developed qualities make up our purpose in this lifetime, we can say our least-developed qualities are our lesson. Your life lesson is the greatest resistance in your life. It is the theme which holds you back from achieving your purpose. These are the things you need to learn to excel in your purpose. You can think of them as opposite sides of the same coin. You can't have one without the other; they work together to create the whole. Simply put, your purpose is what you are here to do, and your lesson is what you need to learn to do it.

Your human experience is an aid to your spiritual development through the mind/body vehicle. With this view, we can focus on our soul as experienced in its journey. Every soul who has entered this human realm has done so with intention. This intention is to discover who you are and your relationship to your greater power. To achieve your soul's intention, you must peel back the layers to reveal your essence.

Through our challenges, we become aware of how our life has guided our evolution. So many times, we blame our environment or our parents for the way we are. In the context of our soul's journey, we picked this particular life to learn and grow. These patterns had begun before you were born. This means every event or circumstance was a necessary part of your development. If you look at these events—some of them possibly being quite traumatic—as an important part of your story, you put them in a more neutral light.

Viewing all aspects of your life as integral to your soul's growth, you can then evaluate them without judgment, gaining insight into the role you played, how you reacted, how you used the event, how the event shaped your future behavior and growth. These are all things which need to be assessed for every facet of your life. You will then begin to see patterns in events and relationships and your actions and reactions to them. These patterns are your life lesson.

To discover what this purpose is for you, begin by creating an awareness of your environment and how you relate to it. Everything is designed to guide your soul's development to your purpose. There is nothing random; everything serves a function.

Your environment and the people you encounter are your mirrors, reflecting your inner self. Through careful observation of who you are and how you relate to this world, you can become aware of your purpose.

You, consciously and unconsciously, create your environment to reflect your internal needs. One of these needs is for your life purpose to be fulfilled.

Story 1
True story: Who Packs Your Parachute?

Charles Plumb was a US Navy jet pilot in Vietnam. After 75 combat missions, his plane was destroyed by a surface-to-air missile. Plumb ejected and parachuted into enemy hands. He was captured and spent six years in a communist Vietnamese prison. He survived the ordeal and now lectures on lessons learned from that experience.

One day, when Plumb and his wife were sitting in a restaurant, a man at another table came up and said, "You're Plumb! You flew jet fighters in Vietnam from the aircraft carrier Kitty Hawk. You were shot down!"

"How in the world did you know that?" asked Plumb.

"I packed your parachute," the man replied. Plumb sat back and gasped in surprise and gratitude. The man pumped his hand and said, "I guess it worked!" Plumb assured him, "It sure did. If your chute hadn't worked, I wouldn't be here today."

Plumb couldn't sleep that night, thinking about that man. Plumb says, "I kept wondering what he might have looked like in a Navy uniform: a white hat, a bib in the back, and bell-bottom trousers. I wonder how many times I might have seen him and not even said 'Good morning, how are you?' or anything because, you see, I was a fighter pilot and he was just a sailor."

Plumb thought of the man hours the sailor had spent at a long wooden table in the bowels of the ship, carefully weaving the shrouds and folding the silks of each chute, holding in his hands, each time, the fate of someone he didn't know.

Now, Plumb asks his audience, "Who's packing your parachute?" Everyone has someone who provides what they need to make it through the day. Plumb also points out he needed many kinds of parachutes when his plane was shot down over enemy territory: he needed his physical parachute, his mental parachute, his emotional parachute, and his spiritual parachute. He called on all these supports before reaching safety.

Sometimes in the daily challenges life gives us, we miss what is important. We may fail to say hello, please, or thank you, congratulate someone on something wonderful that has happened to them, give a compliment, or just do something nice for no reason.

As you go through this week, this month, this year, recognize people who pack your parachute.

I've always had a great respect for those serving in every capacity of our military. The most intriguing combat warriors to me are, without question, the Navy SEALs. Who better to listen to as it relates to lessons learned.

The Seven SEAL Secret Habits
Shared by Brent Gleeson, retired Navy SEAL:

1. **Be loyal.** Team loyalty in the corporate environment seems to be a dying philosophy. Loyalty to the team starts at the top. If it lacks at the senior executive level, how can anyone else in the organization embrace it? Loyalty is about leading by example, providing your team unconditional support, and never throwing a team member under the bus.

2. **Put others before yourself**. Get up every day and ask yourself what you will do to add value to your team, such as simply offering your assistance with a project. The challenge is overcoming the fear your team member might say: "Yes, I need your help with this project... tonight."

3. **Be reflective.** Reflective people often spend too much time analyzing their actions. But imagine if you could harness this talent into something highly valuable? Reflecting on your

mistakes, such as mine in Iraq, ensures you never repeat them.

4. **Be obsessively organized**. Some of us innately have this ability, often to a fault, and some have to work at it a bit more. You have to find a process that works for you. I've known people who will put something on their to-do list after they did it and then cross it off to feel a greater sense of accomplishment! Whatever your system is, make it work for you.

5. **Assume you don't know enough**. Because you don't. Any effective team member understands that training is never complete. It's true in the SEAL teams, and it's true for any elite team. Those who assume they know everything should be eliminated. Those who spend time inside and outside of the workplace developing their knowledge and skills will provide the momentum for their team's forward progress.

6. **Be detail-oriented**. Attention to detail is one of our company's values. Do we get it right all the time? Of course not. Imagine, though, if all members of a team are obsessed with detail in their delivery? My lack of attention to detail in the incident in Iraq could have had catastrophic results. Don't ask yourself what you are going to do today to be successful; ask how you are going to do it.

7. **Never get comfortable.** Always push yourself outside of your comfort zone. If you do this continually with every task you take on, that

boundary will continue to widen. This process will ensure you are continually maximizing your potential, which will positively impact your team.

You may be wondering how you could ever have a relaxed life if you maintain all of these habits. But that's the beauty of it. If you enjoy what you do and form good habits, it all becomes second nature. Maintain these habits, and encourage your team members to do the same. Your lessons will reward you.

Everybody knows the training program Navy SEALs are required to complete is one of the most challenging experiences any human being endure. Only the best of the best of the best survive.

While many may be physically qualified, it's the mental toughness which is the breakthrough ingredient in the end.

Story 2
Personal story...

I've always wondered what it would take and what would it feel like to experience the mental fortitude of a Navy SEAL. In 2014, I had the opportunity to join an elite group of real estate professionals to experience a three-day immersion at the SEALFIT center in Encinitas, CA. It was a rare civilian opportunity to experience an extreme training and education regimen with veteran Navy SEALs.

SEALFIT is a high-level training facility used by prospective Navy SEALs in preparation for BUD/S training.

We understood what the minimum physical requirements were to qualify for the training. Everyone knew it would be physically demanding. For many of us, it proved to be the most physically demanding thing we had ever done. But the real reason many of us committed to this life changing event was to get a glimpse of the mental toughness that differentiates the Navy SEALs from everyone else.

My goal was to experience a mental breakthrough that would take me to another realm of my being and I would not be disappointed. After continuously pushing myself or, rather, being pushed day and night over the course of this long, arduous weekend it came.

On the last day at about 3:00 AM, we were once again marching into the cold black ocean arm-in-arm, and I hit my mental wall. I thought to myself, that's enough! This abuse is over now! Then my mental alarm went off. It was that breakpoint of fight or flight, sink or swim, do or die.

At that moment, my eyes gave a piercing gaze directly into my fear, which was just steps ahead of me. I embraced the darkness and pounding surf which lay just ahead and told myself "I got this! I'm a Freaking Navy SEAL!" Okay, maybe it was different "F" word, and maybe I wasn't even close to being a Navy SEAL, but it didn't matter.

At that moment, I no longer felt the cold, the wind, the pain, the wetness. I felt a surreal energy I had never felt before. It was as if I could carry everybody to the finish line. In my mind, I was bulletproof and unstoppable. I embraced the suck, and my fear disappeared. I felt a calm control while moving and breathing at a different level than ever before.

My lessons from this journey were free flowing through me. It all made sense. I felt a bond with my teammates like I'd never felt with any previous team. That experience is another book in itself. What's important are the lessons I learned. Here are just a few summed up in the words of the SEAL instructors along the way.

Team first. Never quit. Slow is smooth, smooth is fast. Keep calm. Breath, energize, visualize. Pain is weakness leaving the body. Doubt is ended by action alone. Go to know. Get back in the fight. Suffer in Silence. Positive mindset only. See through vision. Fail forward fast. Micro goals. The impossible is possible. Ready to lead, ready to follow. Be prepared. Always know where you're at and where you are going next.

Story 3
Feral Cats

My wife and I like to take our dogs for a walk early in the morning. The dogs seem to look forward to it even more than we do. They especially love to keep a watchful eye out for cats—especially the feral cats in the neighborhood. Recently, after returning from an early morning kayak paddle around the lake near our home, we took the dogs out for their usual walk. I could tell they were a little upset about not being first out that morning. As soon as I opened the side gate to our property, I noticed an open can of what I thought was cat food along with a treat and a small bowl of water.

I thought to myself, "Who would be feeding the feral cats right in front of our gate? Why didn't they put the food by their door?" I grumbled during the whole walk over feral cats being fed at my door by a stranger.

Shortly after returning from the walk and still grumbling around the yard, a neighbor stopped by and shouted over our fence, "Did you get your dog back?" I had no idea what she was talking about, as we had just returned from walking our dogs 10 minutes earlier. While still a little perplexed, I walked over to the side gate to greet her. She proceeded to tell me there was a small brown dog lost outside our gate and she had been trying to save the dog from getting hit by cars on the street earlier that morning. She had put the food, treats, and water in front of our gate, guessing the dog lived there.

It turns out, one of our dogs, being upset that we had the nerve to go kayaking before walking her, had escaped the yard in search of us and was almost hit in rush hour traffic some times. This kind lady had just spent over an hour trying to help our dog, and I had just spent over an hour angry at the person who put food in front of my gate. I felt terrible. Especially since my wife had previously questioned my accusations of some crazy person feeding feral cats in front of my gate while we walked that morning. She told me maybe I had the story wrong in my head. Clearly, a compassionate person with a good heart was trying to be of help for some reason. I didn't want to hear it because I was convinced by my twisted story which was fueled by negative energy.

My judgment was wrong, and I let that negative energy eat at me inside that morning until I found out that the person being helped was me. Lesson learned.

Movie story 4
The Peaceful Warrior

A story about learning lessons...

Dan Millman was a world class gymnast at UC-Berkeley in the mid-1960s. He specialized in the rings earning the nickname "Lord of the Rings."

He worked hard, training seven days a week, fifty weeks out of the year and was on track to make the Olympic team and bring home the Olympic gold, but his constant overthinking, especially having the constant fear it will all be taken away, leads to inconsistency and self-doubt. With his innate skill in a sport he loves, a 4.0 GPA, and all the sex he wants, he knows he should be happy, but in his heart, he knows he isn't.

One of the symptoms of his life is his insomnia. It is during one of his sleepless nights when he meets an older service station operator he sarcastically nicknames Socrates for his philosophical musings. Beyond Socrates' mumbo-jumbo, Dan cannot ignore what appears to be Socrates' almost otherworldly physical feats, something of which Dan can only dream for himself. As such, Dan convinces Socrates to take him under his wing to teach him how to achieve such feats.

At times, Socrates is a reluctant teacher as Dan is not grasping the meaning of what he is trying to convey. Similarly, Dan is sometimes a reluctant pupil not grasping how what Socrates tells him will help him achieve Olympic gold. Through the process, Dan does admit that some of what Socrates imbues in him lead to what Dan views as success. However, it isn't until what Dan strives for the most is threatened in its entirety he becomes fully aware of the gift Socrates provides for him.

Dan's worst fear came true at the worst possible time. It was September 1966, just before his senior year at U.C. Berkeley when his motorcycle collided with a car. He suffered a shattered right femur, requiring surgical repair and bone marrow transplant with a steel nail inserted in his femur. Dan actively pursued rehabilitation with the help of Socrates and was able to return to gymnastics as co-captain of his team and help them win the 1968 NCAA Gymnastics Championships.

In the end, Socrates helped Dan through his brightest and darkest moments. Dan, in turn, learned to embrace his true inner peace, which is at the heart of any warrior.

Some of the best lessons we learn in life come after great struggle. If we believe everything happens for a reason, it can become easier to recognize the silver lining which comes with the painful phases of our journey.

Chapter 4:
"Do the Right Thing"

"Speak the truth even if your voice shakes."

-Unknown

Sometimes doing the right thing comes at a great cost. Here are a couple of true stories about two men who paid a significant price for the right reason.

The Stories of Eddie and Butch:

Eddie's story
Many years ago, Al Capone virtually owned Chicago. Capone wasn't famous for anything heroic. He was notorious for enmeshing the windy city in everything from bootlegged booze and prostitution to murder.

Capone had a lawyer nicknamed "Easy Eddie." He was Capone's lawyer for a good reason. Eddie was very good! In fact, Eddie's skill at legal maneuvering kept Big Al out of jail for a long time. To show his appreciation, Capone paid him very well. Not only was the money big, but Eddie got special dividends, as well. For instance, he and his family occupied a fenced-in mansion with live-in help and all of the conveniences of the day. The estate was so large it filled an entire Chicago City block. Eddie lived the high life of the Chicago mob and gave little consideration to the atrocity going on around him.

Eddie did have one soft spot, however. He had a son he loved dearly. Eddie saw to it his young son had clothes, cars, and a good education. Nothing was withheld. Price was no object. And, despite his involvement with organized crime, Eddie even tried to teach him right from wrong. Eddie wanted his son to be a better man than he was. With all his wealth and influence, there were two things he couldn't give his son; he couldn't pass on a good name or a good example.

One day, Easy Eddie reached a difficult decision. Easy Eddie wanted to rectify wrongs he had done. He decided he would go to the authorities and tell the truth about Al "Scarface" Capone, clean up his tarnished name, and offer his son some semblance of integrity. To do this, he would have to testify against The Mob, and he knew the cost would be great. So, he testified.

Within the year, Easy Eddie's life ended in a blaze of gunfire on a lonely Chicago Street. But in his eyes, he had given his son the greatest gift he had to offer, at the greatest price he could ever pay.

Butch's story:
World War II produced many heroes. One such man was Lieutenant Commander Butch O'Hare. He was a fighter pilot assigned to the aircraft carrier Lexington in the South Pacific.

One day, his entire squadron was sent on a mission. After he was airborne, he looked at his fuel gauge and realized that someone had forgotten to top off his fuel tank. He would not have enough fuel to complete his mission and get back to his ship. His flight leader told him to return to the carrier. Reluctantly, he dropped out of formation and headed back to the fleet.

As he was returning to the mother ship, he saw something that turned his blood cold; a squadron of Japanese aircraft was speeding its way toward the American fleet.

The American fighters were gone on a sortie, and the fleet was all but defenseless. He couldn't reach his squadron and bring them back in time to save the fleet. Nor could he warn the fleet of the approaching danger. There was only one thing to do. He must somehow divert the enemy from the fleet.

Laying aside all thoughts of personal safety, he dove into the formation of Japanese planes. Wing-mounted 50-calibers blazed as he charged in, attacking one surprised enemy plane and then another. Butch wove in and out of the now broken formation and fired at as many planes as possible until all his ammunition was finally spent.

Undaunted, he continued the assault. He dove at the planes, trying to clip a wing or tail in hopes of damaging as many enemy planes as possible, rendering them unfit to fly. Finally, the exasperated Japanese squadron took off in another direction.

Deeply relieved, Butch O'Hare and his tattered fighter limped back to the carrier.

Upon arrival, he reported in and related the events surrounding his return. The film from the gun-camera mounted on his plane told the tale. It showed the extent of Butch's daring attempt to

protect his fleet. He had, in fact, destroyed five enemy aircraft. This took place on February 20, 1942, and for that action, Butch became the Navy's first Ace of WW II, and the first Naval Aviator to win the Congressional Medal of Honor.

A year later, Butch was killed in aerial combat at the age of 29. His home town would not allow the memory of this WW II hero to fade, and today, O'Hare Airport in Chicago is named in tribute to the courage of this great man.

WHAT DO THESE TWO STORIES HAVE TO DO WITH EACH OTHER?

Butch O'Hare was "Easy Eddie's" son.

I always loved this story because it shows that anyone can do the right thing regardless of who they are at any given point in time. There is always hope when there is a heart. When people listen to their heart instead of their head, the right choice can become much more clear.

Personal Story 3

When my kids were young, my wife and I wanted to teach them the value of money and the importance of saving it. One day, we came to an agreement with the kids in which, for every dollar they would invest in a long-term savings account, we would match it, dollar for dollar.

My son thought that was a great idea and diligently saved his money he earned from doing odd jobs or that which he collected for his birthday, Christmas, and special occasions. As time went by, he built a sizable bank account and was proud of his achievement.

One weekend, he had the opportunity to go on a quad riding excursion in the mountains. A quad, as you probably know, is a small four-wheeled all-terrain vehicle. They can be a lot of fun, and they can also be very dangerous. My son borrowed a quad for the adventure from a friend of ours in Flagstaff and was thrilled about the experience he was about to have on the trails in the woods.

At the time, my son thought it would be the greatest thing ever to own a quad, and he let us know he was saving his money to do so. Little did he know at the time, a few major lessons were on the horizon. Late that afternoon, we received a phone call from our friends in Flagstaff. Unfortunately, our son was in an accident. He lost a battle with a large pine tree. Fortunately, he was not injured seriously, having been ejected while the quad wrapped itself around a tree.

The quad was totaled, and the fun was over for him at that moment. Upon returning home, we discussed the importance of doing the right thing. In the end, my son came to the painful conclusion that he should liquidate his savings account he had built up over the recent years and buy our friend a new quad to replace the one destroyed in the accident.

While it broke my heart to see him forfeit his bank account, we knew it was the right thing to do, and it was a lesson which would last a lifetime.

How-to steps towards building integrity and the choice to do the right thing
by Scott Hirschfeld, the education consultant

Many of us see ourselves on a journey through this life, looking to be better people, more valuable to those around us, and more purposeful. On this journey, I have noticed true integrity is hard to find and challenging to live. And, yet, we all have the utmost respect for those who hold to an unmoving standard of doing the right thing.

Some would say integrity is something you have. I have come to believe it is something you choose. We can choose to have integrity and choose to do the things which build our integrity. Integrity is simple as many good things are, but that doesn't mean it is easy. To me, it means choosing the right, honest, and true thing, even to your hurt, embarrassment, or guilt.

Here are five ways to measure and build integrity in your life. Ask yourself:

1. **Is my motivation right?**
Integrity is a quality of being, and often, we fool ourselves into thinking we have it. True integrity is incorruptible. This means we will do the right thing, even if it is not convenient, comfortable, or even looks like it will not produce good results. Self-interest can not motivate true integrity. If I have integrity, I don't do what is right because it benefits me. I do what is right simply because it is right. Integrity, when tested, sets its benefit aside to adhere to what is right. It is a deep inner commitment which does not waiver from its code.

2. **Do my thoughts exhibit integrity?**
Sometimes we choose to say or do what is right, even though our thoughts are actively thinking the wrong thing. Making this purposeful choice is a good thing, but ultimately, we want our thoughts to line up as well. To change who we are, we have to fill our minds with the right things. Zig Ziglar famously said, "Your input determines your outlook. Your outlook determines your output, and your output determines your future." To change ourselves so our thoughts line up and our actions are a natural outflow, it often requires changing our mental channel. Instead of filling our minds with junk, we must put our minds on a healthy diet.

3. **Do I do what I say?**

A person of integrity will insist on meeting their commitments. This insistence may force one to learn because good intentions don't necessarily produce the right results. For instance, I may commit to certain actions during a meeting, but if I have not learned to take notes, transfer tasks to a calendar slot and set aside to work on them, and then actually have the discipline to work on them, my integrity is in question. Interestingly enough, if you are committed to doing what you say you will, it changes what you say you will do. We begin to weigh more carefully whether a task is important and whether it will fit with our other commitments.

4. **How do I spend my free time?**

Often, you can measure your integrity by how you spend your free time. What do you watch? What do you read? How do you play? We are all intrigued by the train wreck on TV or in our news feed, but what you fill your mind with is bound to come out in your words, thoughts, and actions. It is hard to keep a positive attitude when you feed on the negative. Replace the negative with learning or volunteering in a way which helps others. You will be amazed at the difference it will make.

5. **Do I start from a position of trust with others?**

People who have an underlying distrust for others often do so because they are not trustworthy themselves. We assume others are like us. If I do not have integrity, then I assume others lack integrity as well. This isn't always true. Some have been hurt so deeply by others; they have a hard time trusting. However, if you find yourself starting from the point of distrust with people, consider your level of trustworthiness. Try to wipe the slate clean and start with trust. Sure, we have to use good judgment, but when we start by trusting others, they have a chance to live up to our expectations, and great things can happen!

Self-interest is the enemy of integrity, so be on guard. When we choose contrary to integrity, we act to protect ourselves. We operate from fear rather than purpose. We choose to hide the truth and protect ourselves. We choose the easy path, rather than the right one.

Movie Story 4
Erin Brockovich

Desperate for work, unskilled Erin Brockovich, single parent of three, takes a relatively inconsequential job as a legal assistant in a California law firm for low wages. While organizing some paperwork about real estate cases, she is puzzled when she notices medical records in one of the files. On a whim, she does a little investigating of her own and comes to suspect that land purchased by Pacific Gas and Electric (PG&E) is the same land on which chromium contamination resulted from PG&E's environmentally irresponsible actions.

Examination of local water records and interviews with residents ill from exposure to poisonous chromium confirm Erin's suspicions, but the pursuit of legal proceedings against PG&E would seem beyond the capabilities of the small law firm where she works. Still, Erin succeeds in making her boss, Ed Masry, as passionate about the case as she is, and he takes it on. Both Ed and Erin must make great sacrifices in their lives, as the legal costs spread Ed very thin, and the round-the-clock work takes Erin out of touch with both her boyfriend and her kids.

Erin's kids resent the lack of attention from her, and her attempts to explain the merits of what she is doing to her eldest son are futile, but one day, her eldest son happens across one of the many documents about the PG&E case. He reads of a child his age who is very ill and knowing Erin's work will help this child, asks her why the child's mother cannot provide the needed help. When Erin explains, it is because the child's mother is very ill, too, her son, for the first time, appreciates the nature and importance of Erin's work.

In the end, Erin's special ability to bond with the victims of chromium contamination and their families and Ed's legal and administrative prowess are the key ingredients to making the case against PG&E. As a team, they manage to successfully lay the groundwork for the payment of legal damages by PG&E to those harmed.

We Are All Souls Having a Human Experience

Image the idea that we are all wonderful eternal souls on earth having a temporary human experience.

What if you knew your greatest power lies within you and this special force that exists within you is always ready to give you whatever you want and all you have to do is know how to tap it.

I love the thought that we are all here to learn and integrate our learning in life. We each have the power inside us to take the formless and put it into form.

Perhaps the real gift comes when we share and teach others life lessons from our own experiences. Maybe that's when the magic really happens.

You are exactly where you are suppose to be right now. I wish you a greater sense of awareness in your life each day and the ability to act upon it.

I encourage you to begin each day with a rampage of gratitude. Before you get out of bed think of 10 or 20 things big and small that your are grateful for in your life right now. Then start your day with a morning ritual focused on your health and well being...walking, running, yoga, meditation, journaling, reading, eating healthy... whatever it is that works for you, do it.

When you take care of your mental and physical health you can better take care of others and live the life you were born to experience.

If this book has in some way helped you find something inside yourself that maybe you didn't recognize before then I encourage you to take the next step which just might take you to a whole new level of awareness from this point forward. Share your soul inspiration.

Please take a moment on Facebook and visit www.facebook.com/SoulGuideInsights. Here you will find a safe harbor of like-minded people sharing their thoughts, messages and experiences.

Know that you are a great soul with many gifts to give and receive. I invite you to be a part of the Soul Guide Tribe and enrich your life along with that of others.

Thank you for taking the time to read this book and open your mind to new possibilities.

The 4 Secrets Towards Mastering Life's Journey...

Have you ever sat and wondered how people can go through the same exact experience and yet have two vastly different opinions on it? You are at, say, an outdoor concert. One person sits in awe of how great the music is and singing and tapping their toe and couldn't be happier. Two blankets over sit a couple who do nothing but complain about the line to the bathroom and the price of the food, and they worry about how much traffic there will be getting home, so they pack up and leave before intermission.

Same experience, two very different outcomes. That's one of the beautiful things about life's journey. We all have the opportunity to create our happiness and success with the thoughts we have and the attitude we bring to everything we do.

Allen Rebenstorf shares his *Soul Guide* secrets with you to help enable you to, as he says, "Choose Happiness." Part *Chicken Soup for the Soul*, part Navy SEAL kick in the butt, Allen's *Soul Guide* will provide a lifetime of insights, wisdom; and he will challenge your status quo, so you are always working on mastering your journey.

About The Author

Allen Rebenstorf is a professional Real Estate Consultant in the Phoenix area. He makes his home in Gilbert, Arizona.

Prior to his real estate career he worked in the Pharmaceutical industry for 20 years and retired from Johnson & Johnson in 2007.

Allen graduated from Arizona State University with degrees in Marketing, Economics and International Business. His wife Beth and his children Shane and Sydney are also ASU alumni.

You can usually find Allen on a beach or a motorcycle adventure when he is not helping friends and clients get from where they are to where they want to be. Look for more "Soul Guide" insights to follow.

54090688R00042

Made in the USA
San Bernardino, CA
07 October 2017